Made in the USA
Las Vegas, NV
08 May 2022

48608430R00070